zendoodle coloring presents

deluxe edition

KEEP MERRY AND COLOR ON

75 yuletide designs

ST. MARTIN'S GRIFFIN
NEW YORK

ZENDOODLE COLORING PRESENTS DELUXE EDITION
KEEP MERRY AND COLOR ON: 75 YULETIDE DESIGNS
Copyright © 2016 by St. Martin's Press. All rights reserved.
Printed in the United States of America. For information, address
St. Martin's Press, 175 Fifth Avenue, New York, N.Y. 10010.

www.stmartins.com

ISBN 978-1-250-11299-6 (trade paperback)

Our books may be purchased in bulk for promotional, educational,
or business use. Please contact your local bookseller or the
Macmillan Corporate and Premium Sales Department at
1-800-221-7945, extension 5442, or by e-mail at
MacmillanSpecialMarkets@macmillan.com.

First Edition: October 2016

10 9 8 7 6 5 4 3 2

Merry Christmas!

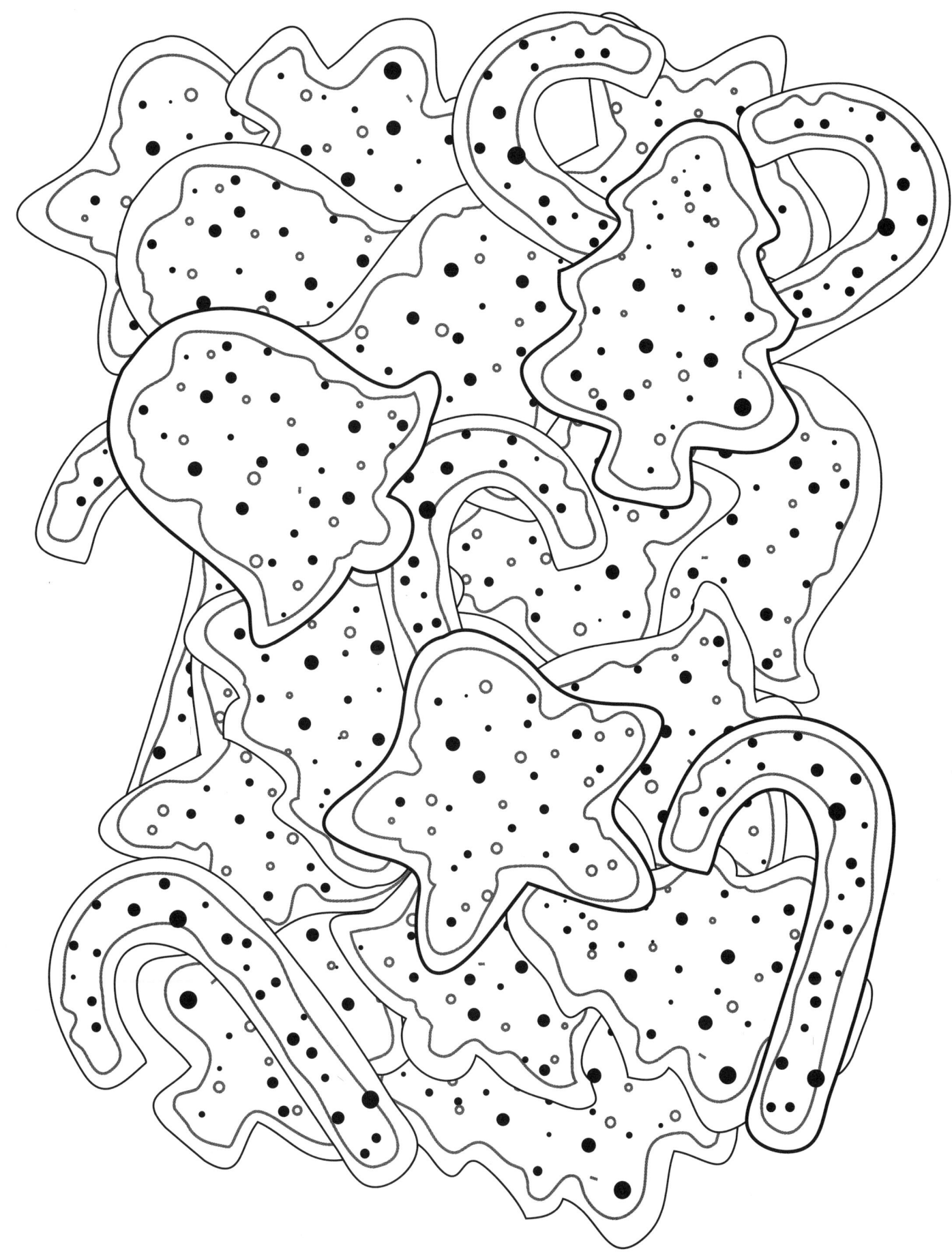

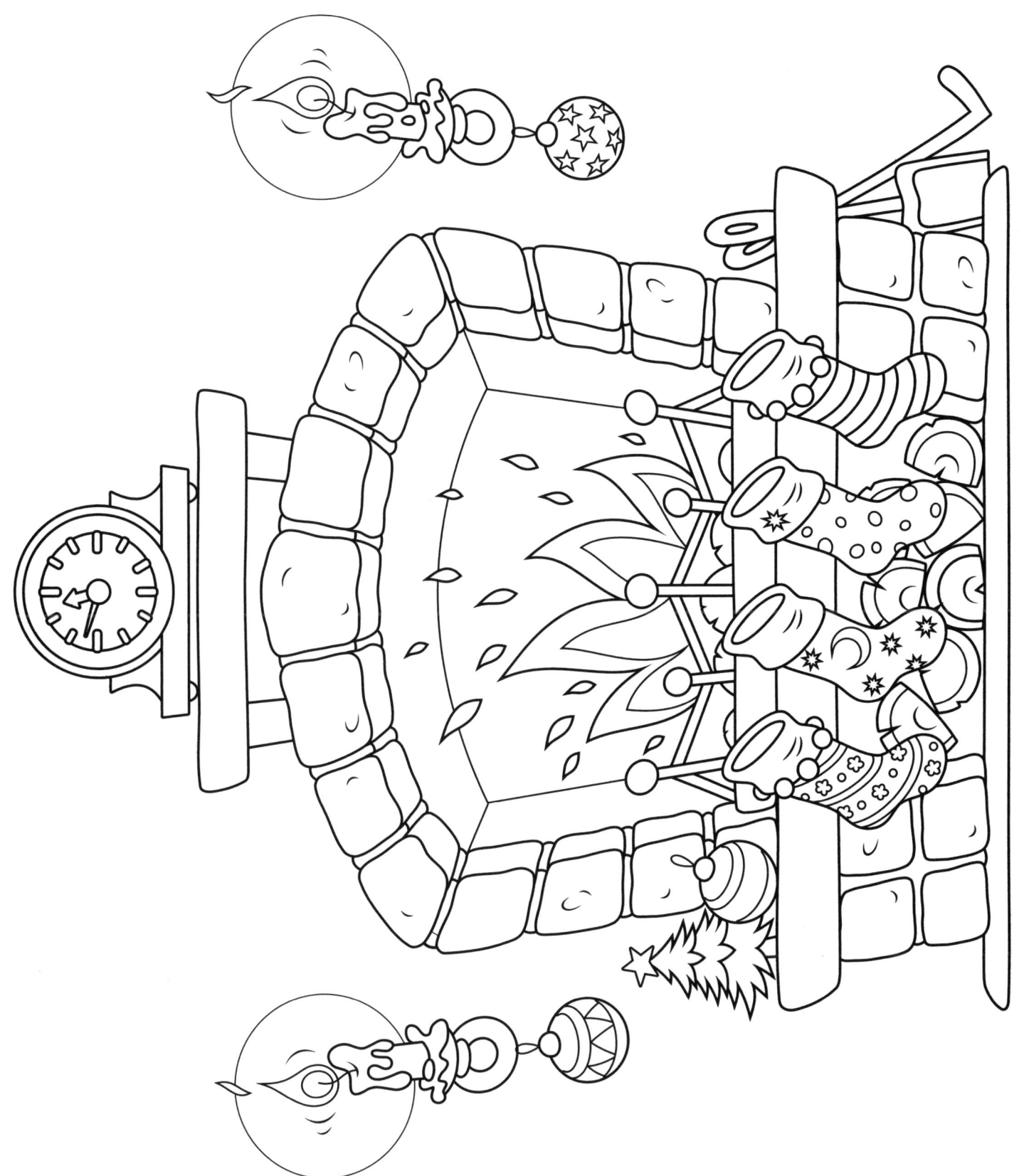

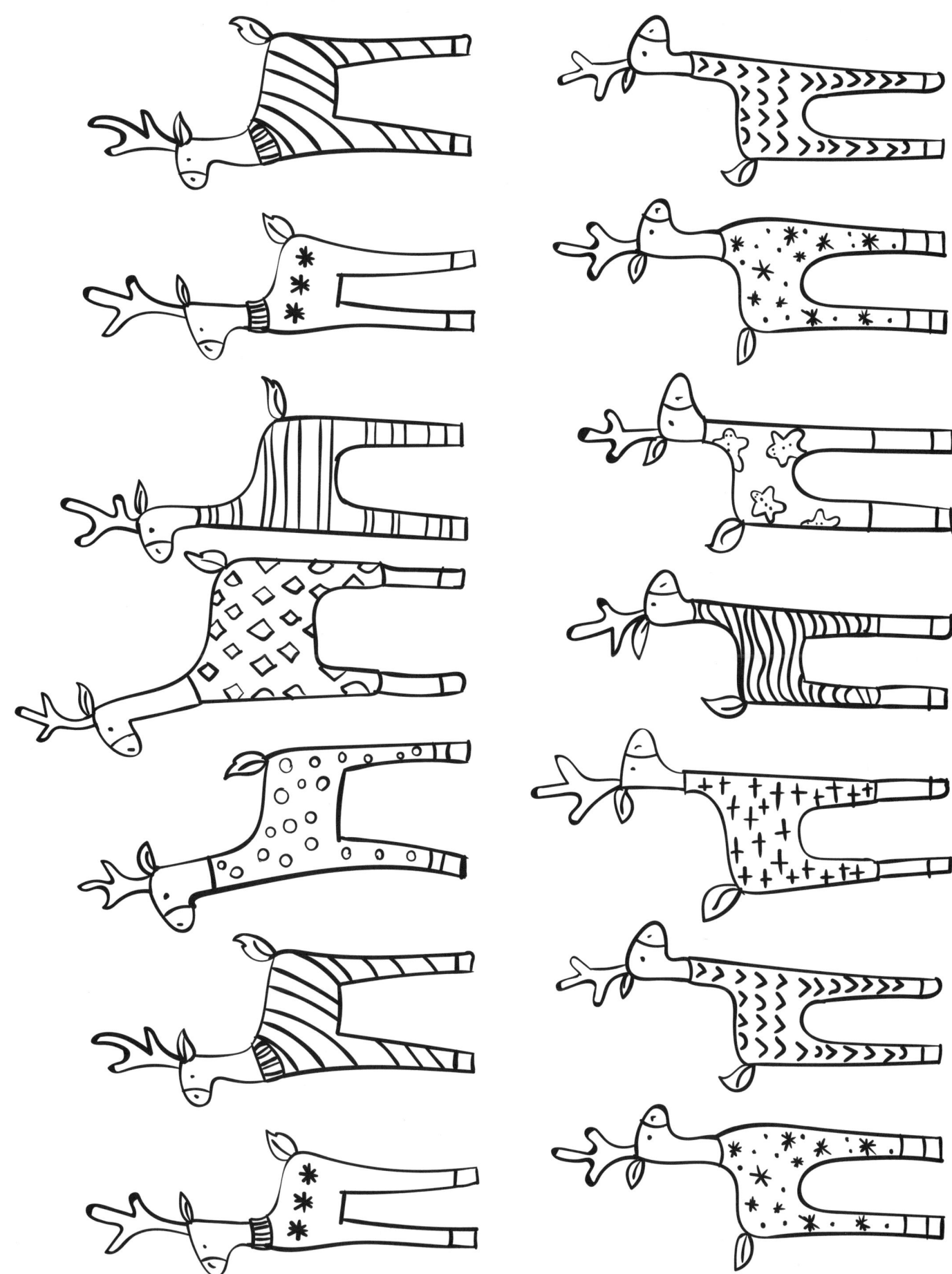

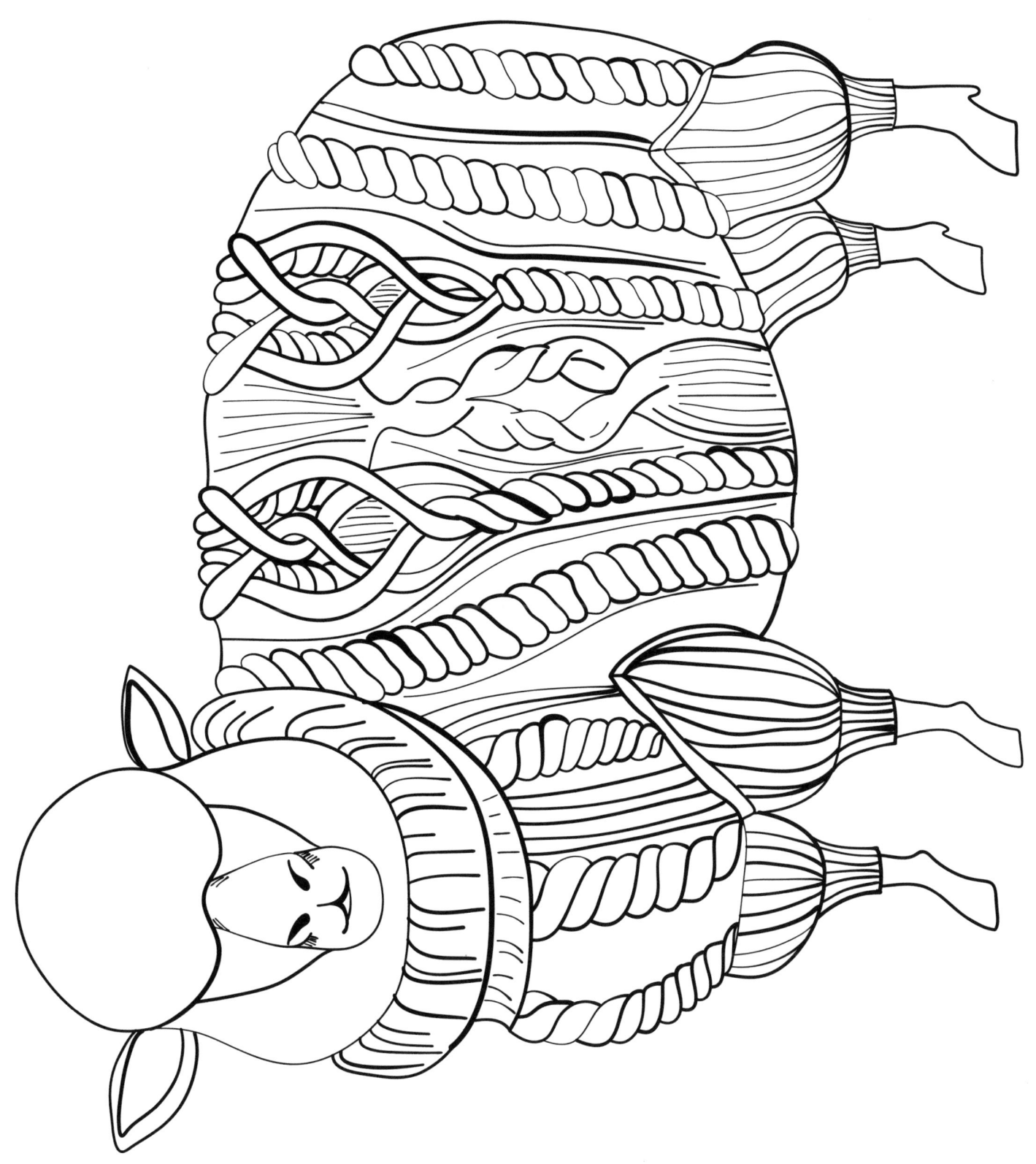

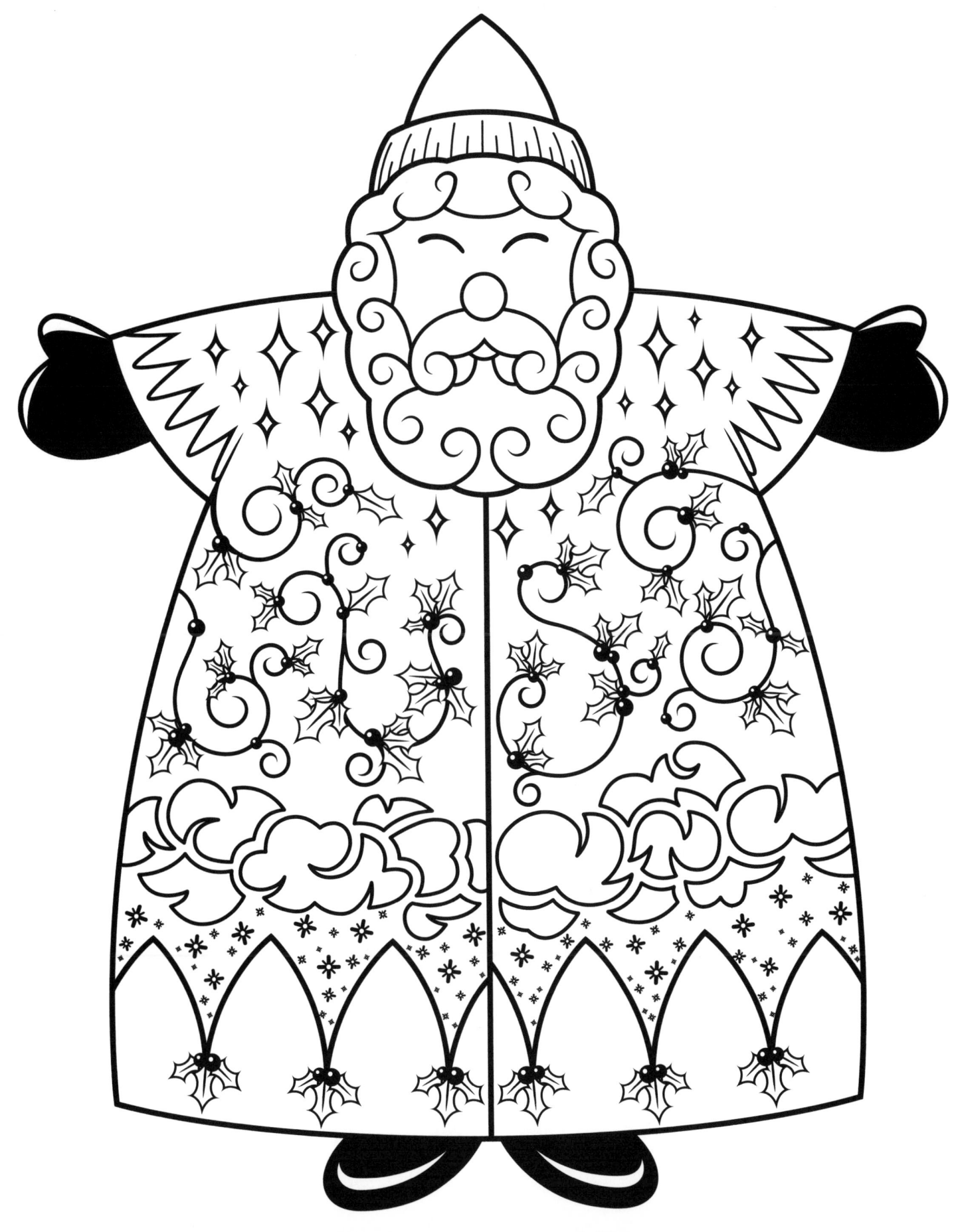

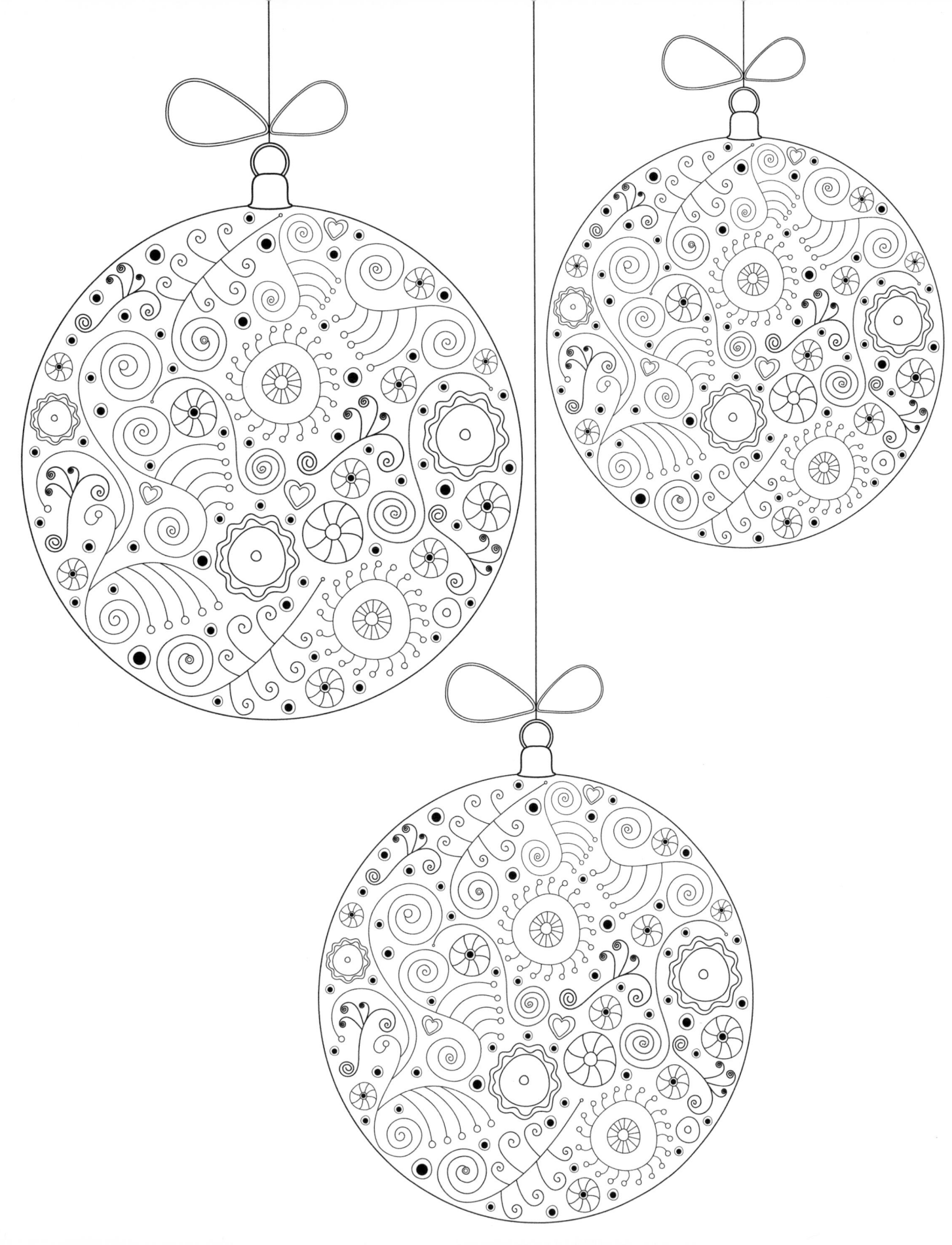

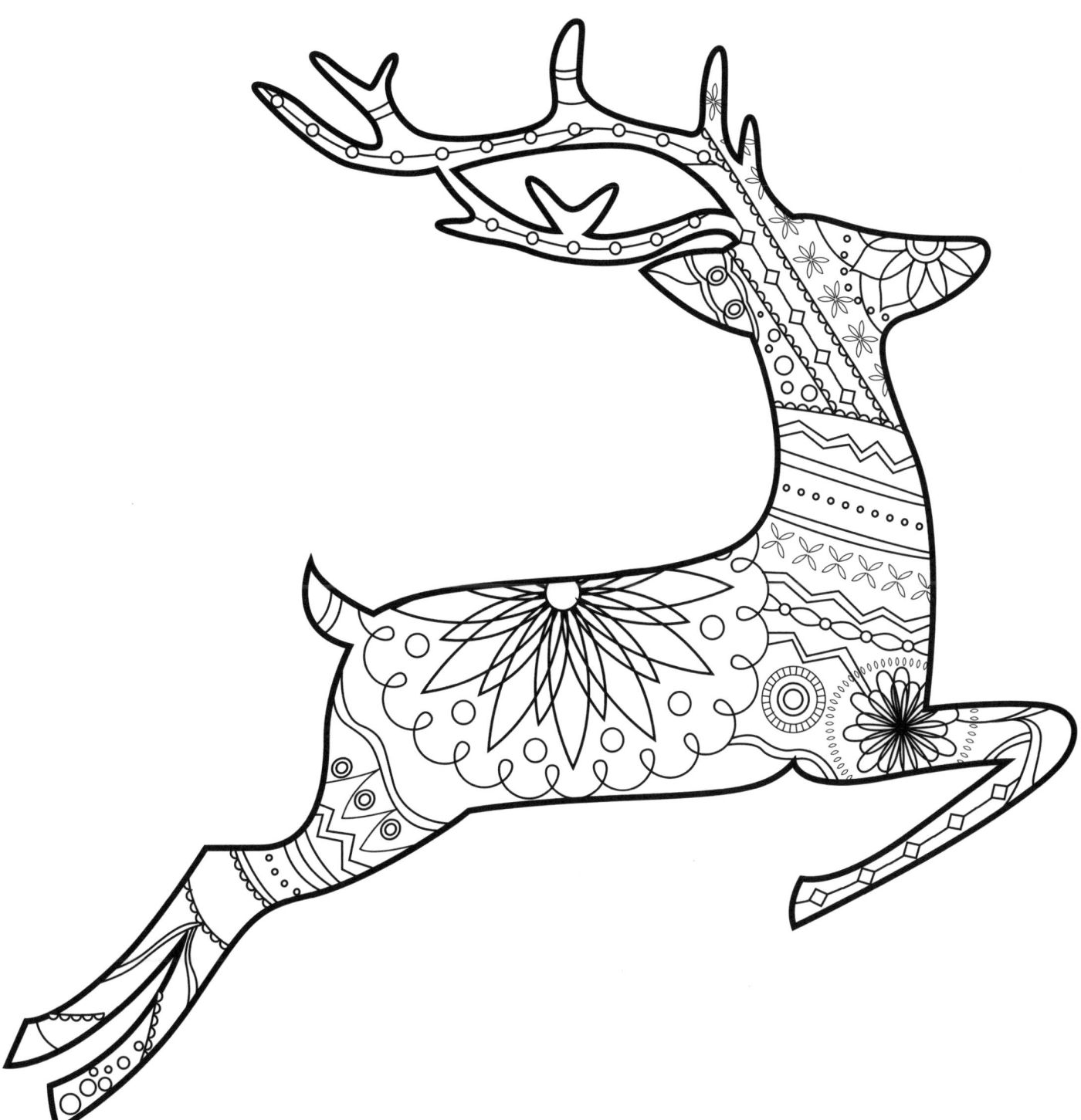

Merry Christmas!

Merry Christmas

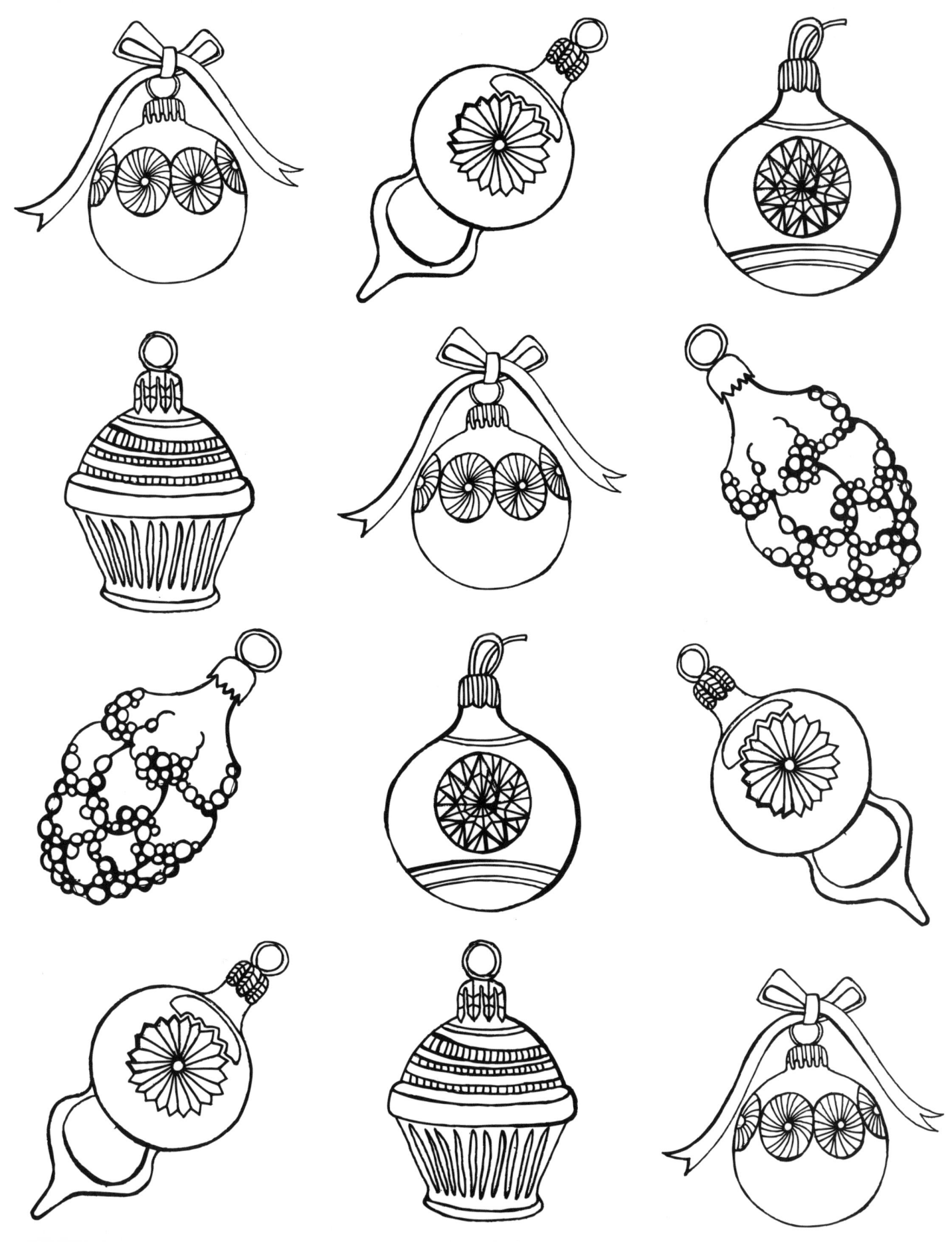

Mistletoe

NORTH POLE

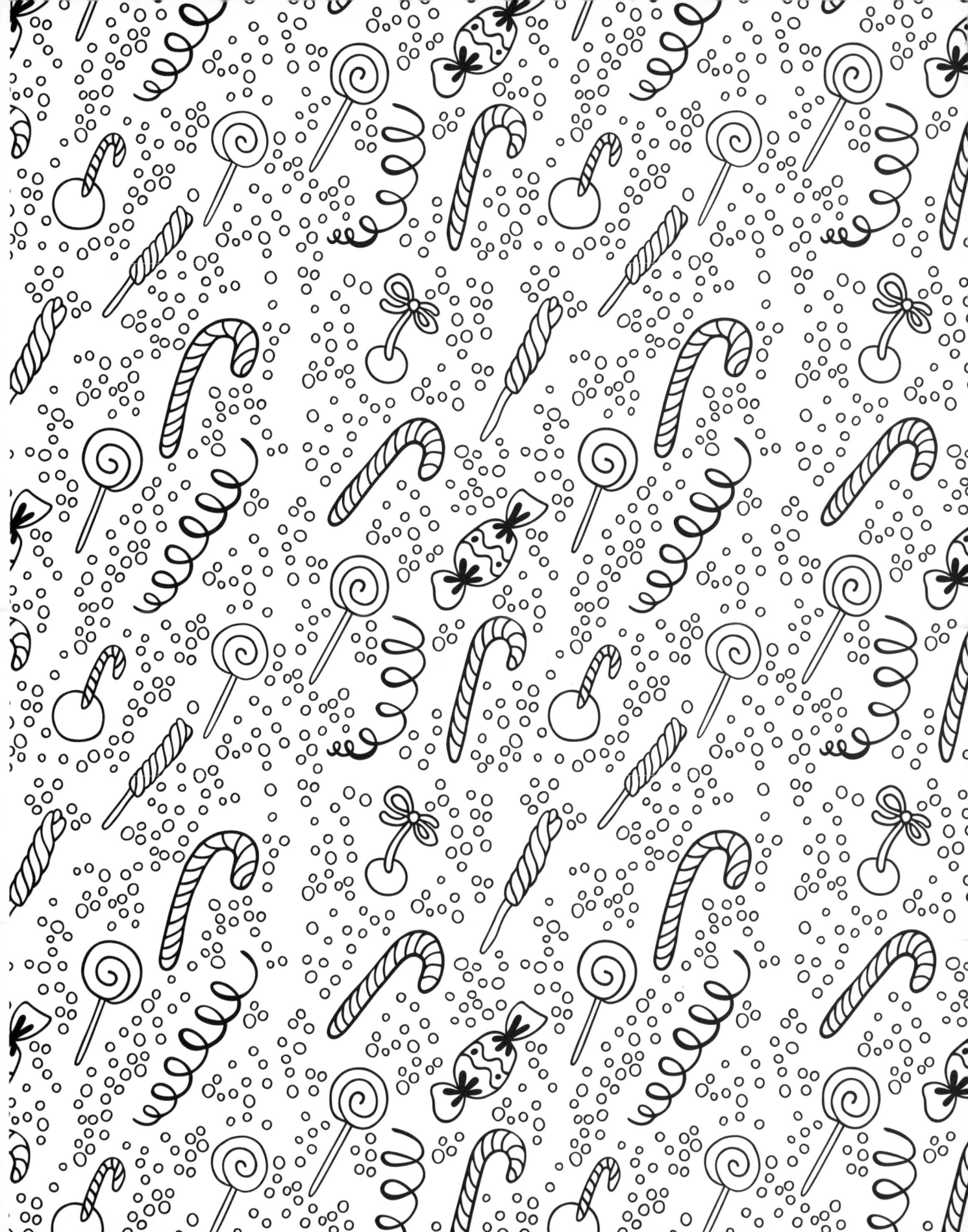